H

Stop Being Busy, Take a Break and Get Better Results While Doing Less

By Martin Meadows

Download another Book for Free

I want to thank you for buying my book and offer you another book (just as long and valuable as this book), *Grit: How to Keep Going When You Want to Give Up*, completely free.

Visit the link below to receive it:

http://www.profoundselfimprovement.com/relax

In *Grit*, I'll share with you how exactly to stick to your goals according to peak performers and science.

In addition to getting *Grit*, you'll also have an opportunity to get my new books for free, enter giveaways and receive other valuable emails from me.

Again, here's the link to sign up:

http://www.profoundselfimprovement.com/relax

Table of Contents

Download another Book for Free 2
Table of Contents 3
Prologue 4
Chapter 1: Your Rituals Create Your Life 7
Chapter 2: Let Your Body Recharge 18
Chapter 3: Get Away from It All to Regain Energy 35
Chapter 4: Let It Go 46
Chapter 5: Seven Habits to Reduce Stress 56
Epilogue 70
Bonus: How to Get Results without Being Busy 73
Download another Book for Free 82
Could You Help? 83
About Martin Meadows 84

Prologue

Have you ever stopped in the middle of a busy street and looked at the crowd?

Could you feel the stress and tension by just looking at these people?

Don't you find it terrifying how out of hand busyness has become in today's world?

There are people working over twelve hours every single day, falling asleep in the metro. There are overstressed parents who can't afford to spend time with their own kids. There are people in their twenties neglecting every single aspect of their lives but their career.

One person out of four dies from cardiovascular disease[i] caused mostly by unhealthy eating, a lack of physical activity, smoking and consuming too much alcohol, even though it's preventable in 90% of the cases.

What's the most common escape route for busy, overworked people? They stuff themselves with worthless junk food that clogs their arteries. They drown their emotions in alcohol. They smoke a pack or two a day.

I have never wanted to be a part of this crowd, hence I spent a lot of time researching and optimizing every aspect of my life to avoid the same fate. Philosophy of *less is more* guides my life, keeping me sane and healthy in the fast-moving world.

In this part, you'll learn why busyness is wrong and how to:

- step away from noise and the neck-breaking speed of the world around you,

- recharge your overstressed mind and body,

- deal with nagging, negative emotions,

- utilize some of the most effective stress-reducing habits,

- and achieve a lot despite not being part of the overworked crowd.

Please keep in mind I'm not a doctor. Although the advice presented in this part is based on scientific research and experts, it can't replace professional medical care. If you suffer from any conditions that require professional care (hypertension, diabetes, etc.), do not follow my advice until your physician allows it.

If you suffer from mental health disorders, this book won't cure you. I wrote it for people who want to learn how to transition to a slower, healthier life, not as a guide for dealing with stress disorders. I'm by no means a psychologist – consider this book more as a piece of advice from a curious mind.

Now that we got the disclaimers out of the way, let's talk about the first step to regain control over your life. I believe it's the key ingredient that has to be a part of your everyday life if you want to slow down.

Chapter 1: Your Rituals Create Your Life

There's no need to tell you why stress (the negative kind) is bad. It's well-documented how dangerous it is to your mental and physical health, and why it's so important to avoid it.

You've also read about healthy eating and regular exercise in numerous books and articles, haven't you? I'm not here to tell you obvious things.

What is frequently downplayed, though, is the importance of your rituals. By rituals, I don't mean habits like exercising three times per week or flossing. I'm talking about creating an empowering structure of your day, of which the most important part is what you do in the morning.

For years, I didn't have a proper morning ritual. Consequently, I started each day reacting to the world. There was no time for introspection in the morning, and it's easy to forget to stop for a second during the day.

If you wake up and don't feel control over your day, guess how it will influence the rest of your waking hours.

The first step to stop being so busy and overwhelmed during the day is to…

Develop Your Morning Routine

The state in which you start your day shapes your state of mind for the entire day.

If you wake up groggy, stressed out thinking whether you can make it to work (or your home office) on time, and reacting to the events happening around you (your spouse reminding you to pick the kid up from school, your hungry son waiting for breakfast, your cat meowing for food, and your dog barking for a walk), you enter a reactive, restless state of mind that will guide you the entire day.

It's almost as if busyness is a little monster waking up with you, following you from the moment you get up to the moment you go to sleep again. "Hey, do this!" "You need to do that!" "That requires your attention now!" It's croaking into your ear from the second you open your eyes, and off you go, like an obedient dog.

Fortunately, there's a simple solution to this problem: wake up 20 minutes earlier and perform your morning ritual.

A proper morning routine should consist of activities that will clear your mind and help you calm down before you enter the frenzy of busyness and let it ravage your mind.

Slow Down and Get More Oxygen

Meditation is one of the keys to an empowering, calming morning routine.

A meta-analysis of 47 studies on meditation shows that meditation can reduce psychological stress and improve mental health-related quality of life[ii]. The simple act of sitting still and focusing on your breath can decrease the symptoms of depression, anxiety, and even alleviate pain.

For some people, meditation is associated with discomfort because they tried it once or twice and couldn't calm their inner monologue. If you have a similar experience, don't skip this chapter thinking you're not good at meditation. A racing mind happens to everyone new to meditation.

The key to implementing meditation in your life is to start small. Even if you meditate for just five minutes a day, the mere practice will reduce your stress – even if your thoughts are jumping from one thing to another the entire time.

I had always wondered how to meditate, but the books about it were lengthy and made it a highly spiritual, difficult thing to do. Turns out meditation is much simpler than most people believe, and no lengthy book is needed to master it (although it can help you if you want to learn more about it).

The key in meditation is to focus on the present moment and the sensations traveling through your body while you sit still. Here's a simple step-by-step explanation of how to do it.

1. Sit still in a comfortable position

Don't stand up, don't lie down – sit with an upright posture. Some proponents of meditation practice meditation while standing up or lying down, but for most people it's not a good idea. If you suffer from back pain or other conditions that prevent you from sitting upright for a few minutes, then consider lying flat on your back.

Unless you're super flexible, forget about the cross-legged lotus position you've seen in movies and photos. The three most common and easiest positions for beginners are:

- sitting on the edge of a chair with your back straight. Your back has to be straight, unsupported by the chair. It can be as simple as that, though I find it more tiring than other positions.

- sitting cross-legged. It's easy and common among beginners. Sitting on a pillow will make it more comfortable. I find it too straining for my back, hence I prefer the third option:

- *seiza* position. Fold your legs underneath your thighs and rest your buttocks on your heels. For more comfort, you can put a pillow under your rear.

Try all of these positions and find out which one works best for you. If you're so inclined, get a meditation seat or cushion.

Set an alarm on your phone (just don't use an obnoxious, loud alarm that will give you a heart attack) or better yet, use a meditation app. At first, three to five minutes is more than enough.

2. Close your eyes and focus on your breathing

Simple counting – one (inhale), two (exhale), one (inhale), two (exhale) works best. You can also count each breath until you reach 100. At first, don't expect to reach more than 20 before you lose your concentration. Don't get angry – just start again from 0.

Once you get better at maintaining focus, you can stop counting your breaths and focus on the general feeling of relaxation spreading through your body.

3. Focus on the sensations in your body as you inhale and exhale

Start from your feet and go upward, trying to relax every little muscle. Lose tension in your feet, calves, thighs, hips, stomach, arms, hands, fingers, neck, jaw, and so on.

You'll be surprised how much tension you store in certain parts of your body – including tension in the places you weren't aware of before, such as your chin.

If you lose your focus, bring it back to your breathing and the sensations in your body. Don't get discouraged. It's a part of the process.

Repeat the practice every single morning.

Don't make your sessions longer until you become comfortable sitting still for five minutes. It's better to add an additional minute every other week or so (or add a second session in the day), rather than get discouraged when you find yourself unable to focus.

Note you can also use meditative techniques during your day. Each time you get distracted, return to your breathing, regain focus and go back to what you were doing. Over time, your default response to getting distracted will be focusing on your breathing instead of on the distraction.

What Are the Next Steps After Meditation?

Meditation will put you in a calmer, more introspective state of mind. The second part of the ritual should incorporate some kind of positive thinking to get negative, nagging thoughts out of your head.

I recommend a simple practice of expressing gratitude and appreciation for what you have. Various studies show that gratitude improves well-being and helps maintain positive mood[iii, iv, v]. Moreover, gratitude strengthens our relationships with our partners[vi], improves connection and satisfaction with them[vii], and is important to maintain intimate bonds[viii].

Each morning, think of three to five things (or more, if you want) for which you're grateful. It takes seconds, and the positive state you'll enter thanks to this simple practice will tremendously improve your mood. Don't underestimate the power of gratitude – it's more impactful than you believe.

After meditation and gratitude, review your personal documents detailing your vision and most important goals for the next months. Don't have them yet? Write them down as soon as possible (Tony Robbins' book *Unlimited Power*[ix] is a good starting point if you don't know how to do it).

It's also a good idea to review your most important plans for the day, or for the week. The knowledge of what you need to achieve will make you feel more in control.

If you have some time left, spend a few minutes reading an inspirational book or reviewing any other material that makes you feel in control and ready for the day.

Cherish your quiet time in the morning. Prepare yourself for the day ahead by meditation, express gratitude and get inspired. Your days will, almost magically, become much more manageable.

YOUR RITUALS CREATE YOUR LIFE: QUICK RECAP

1. How you start your day affects how you're going to feel later on. If you start your day in a rush, your entire day will feel rushed. If you start it more slowly, you'll feel less overwhelmed and busy.

2. Start waking up at least 20 minutes earlier to start your day the right way. You shouldn't rush your morning ritual.

3. Meditation is one of the keys to enter the positive state of mind and prepare yourself for the day ahead. Start with three to five minutes of sitting still and focusing on your breath. Relax your muscles, refocus each time you lose your concentration, and enjoy the process.

4. Gratitude is crucial to a happy life. If you start your day expressing appreciation and gratitude for what you already have, you'll uplift yourself and be better prepared for the day awaiting you.

5. Each morning, re-read your personal vision and review your short-term goals. Read Tony

Robbins' book *Unlimited Power* if you don't know how to do it.

6. Reviewing your plans and reading inspirational books will get you in a more resourceful and confident state of mind.

Chapter 2: Let Your Body Recharge

Your body dictates how you feel internally. If you don't take the time to recharge it, sooner or later the effects of abuse will creep into other areas of your life. If you're reading this book, chances are it has already done so.

As I already mentioned in the first chapter, I'm not here to tell you how to eat healthy or how often you have to exercise. I want to share with you more unconventional or lesser-known tips to help you recharge and take more control over your life.

There are three main techniques for recharging I want to discuss:

The Myth of a Sleep-Deprived Hero

Sleep deprivation is more common than you think, and its effects are much more terrifying than most people believe. A week of sleeping four or five hours per night (a deficit of about 24–30 hours of sleep) is equal to an impairment caused by four to five glasses of beer. Two weeks of sleeping four to five hours per night makes the symptoms double.

Some people like to brag how little they sleep, essentially bragging they're drunk every single day. 1,550 deaths and 71,000 injuries a year are the needless result of sleep deprivation[x].

When your body craves more sleep, your attention, alertness, concentration, and problem solving are all impaired. You learn less effectively and are more likely to be depressed. Your skin ages more quickly. With long-term sleep deprivation, you're more likely to be obese[xi].

There are two ways to battle sleep deprivation – sleep longer during the night or take naps (ideally, use both techniques).

Sleeping longer is obvious – you need to make time for more sleep.

Naps are trickier and require experimentation. Power naps of 15 to 20 minutes are generally most common and provide best results in studies[xii]. Naps that are longer than 30 minutes are as recharging as shorter naps, but it takes longer to feel the benefits (and you'll wake up groggy). A full 90-minute cycle of sleep is most beneficial in terms of recharging your body.

Try different durations to test which one works best for you. For me, naps of 15 to 20 minutes don't work because I need at least 15 minutes to fall asleep. If I'm tired, I usually take a longer, 90-minute nap, fully prepared to feel groggy for the first 15 to 30 minutes after waking up (and then fantastic an hour or so later once the benefits kick in).

There's also another, relatively common reason why you can feel tired after the night – you sleep too long and confuse your body. Some people sleep too little during the week and too long during the weekend. Aim for seven to nine hours of sleep every single day instead of five to six hours during the week and ten to twelve during the weekend.

It's also important to note that often you can get enough sleep, but still suffer from sleep deprivation because the quality of your sleep is low. The main factors that influence your sleep quality are:

1. Sleep schedule

Going to sleep and waking up at the same time (even on the weekends) will regulate your body's clock and help you fall asleep more quickly and wake up more easily.

2. Your bedroom

The most beneficial temperature for sleep is 60-67 degrees Fahrenheit (15-19 Celsius)[xiii]. Your bedroom should be dark and as quiet as possible. Consider using curtains, eye shades, and ear plugs to get a better quality of sleep.

3. Your mattress

If it's been longer than 10 years since you last changed your mattress, it's time to invest in a new one. There are many different types of mattresses suitable for different people. Speak with an expert to learn which mattress will work best for you. When testing a mattress, give it at least fifteen minutes before you decide how comfortable it feels.

4. Blue light

Blue light emitted by electronics and energy-efficient lightbulbs suppresses melatonin (hormone regulating sleep and wake cycles) and shifts your circadian rhythms. If you always use electronics before sleep, you'll find it harder to fall asleep.

Since it's highly unlikely you can turn off all your devices and light two to three hours before going to sleep, consider investing in dim red lights for night lights. Red light has the least power to shift circadian rhythm and suppress melatonin[xiv].

You can also buy blue-blocking glasses – especially if you use a lot of electronic devices before sleep.

Exposing yourself to bright light during the day (the more, the better) will improve your ability to fall asleep at night. Consider adding a short walk to your daily routine.

5. Your racing mind

If you're one of the hyperactive people who can't stop thinking while trying to fall asleep, write down all your thoughts in a notepad. The mere act of writing down your thoughts can be enough to calm your racing mind and fall asleep sooner.

6. Caffeine

Drinking coffee or tea before sleep is a sure-fire way to make yourself unable to sleep or have poor quality sleep. Caffeine-induced sleep disorder is the term used for those who consume too much caffeine and can't sleep.

Caffeine will persist in your body for 3 to 7 hours[xv]. To stay on the safe side, stop drinking any caffeinated beverages 7 to 8 hours before going to sleep.

7. Your diet

Heavy meals in the evening can make it hard to sleep. Stop eating two to three hours before going to sleep to avoid the discomfort of disrupted sleep or the inability to fall asleep altogether.

Let Your Body Repair Itself

In today's world with food available everywhere at a moment's notice, five to seven meals a day are a norm. Breakfast, brunch, lunch, dinner, snacks – most people eat every other hour or so and let their digestive systems rest only for a few hours during the night. 10% of obese people have an overpowering urge to eat at night[xvi], leading to an eating disorder called night eating syndrome.

For years, I've been fasting every single day for at least 16 to 20 hours, and sometimes up to 40 hours. I don't remember the last time I felt ravenous hunger the way I felt it when I ate three to five meals a day. My health and fitness have only improved since I switched my eating pattern. I no longer envision myself going back to numerous smaller meals during the day. Fasting has become a way of life for me.

I don't claim fasting to be the cure-it-all solution, though. I don't believe fasting is the right choice for all people. However, as long as you don't suffer from any medical conditions that make fasting dangerous without proper care (e.g., diabetes), I believe it's an experiment worth trying.

Let me explain why, and what it has to do with recharging yourself.

When animals are sick or injured, they fast (while drinking ample amounts of water) to let their bodies heal. Digestion requires energy that could be used to restore your body and heal itself. Studies show that fasting triggers the process of autophagy[xvii] and possibly also apoptosis, breaking down and rebuilding dysfunctional components like proteins, organelles and cells. In essence, it's rebuilding the building blocks of your body and rejuvenating the entire organism.

What a shame that most humans rarely, if ever, do it, thus prolonging their recovery and never letting their bodies properly repair.

Studies show that intermittent fasting – cycling between a period of fasting and non-fasting – has beneficial effects on the cardiovascular and cerebrovascular systems[xviii]. It's also beneficial for successful brain aging[xix]. If you're afraid you won't be as creative or effective when fasting, studies show that it doesn't reduce your cognitive performance, sleep or mood[xx].

Contrary to common knowledge, you don't need to eat five meals a day to lose fat[xxi] or stave off hunger[xxii]. Quite the contrary – alternate-day fasting (fasting every other day) may encourage fat oxidation[xxiii]. It can also reduce body weight, levels of bad cholesterol, LDL, and triglyceride levels[xxiv].

As long as you're healthy, there's no reason why you shouldn't try experimenting with fasting. There are several approaches you can consider:

1. Shorten the window you're eating to 4–8 hours a day. It's my pattern of eating – fasting for 16 to 20 hours and eating in a 4–8-hour window. This approach is most beneficial for athletes and bodybuilders who can structure their meals around their workout.

2. The more universal approach is to designate one or two non-consecutive days during the week when you fast for 24 hours. By following this approach, you stop eating at, say, 6 PM, and resume eating at 6 PM the next day, skipping breakfast and dinner.

3. A more difficult approach for most people is to skip an entire day of eating. For instance, you eat normally for six days, and then don't eat anything on Sunday. You resume eating on Monday morning, thus

effectively making your fast a 36-hour or so period of not eating.

Fasting doesn't have to be scary. If you find the prospect of not eating for 16 to 20 hours (or longer) daunting, start small. Skip breakfast or eat your last meal two to four hours sooner (you won't feel hunger when you sleep). Remember to drink a lot of water (and any other non-caloric beverages, including tea and black coffee).

By giving your digestive system a break, you'll give your body an opportunity to recharge and rebuild itself.

Your Muscles Are Tenser than You Think

Back pain and other little pains are a default physical state for many people –most notably overworked office workers who get little to no physical exercise (who, in today's world, make up a large part of society).

Chances are your entire body is rigid and tense, causing you pain every single day. It's not only physical pain we're talking about – inflexibility and decreased range of motion will also affect your mental health.

Your physiology reflects your state of mind. A single massage therapy session can almost instantly change your state from overstressed and exhausted to refreshed and happy.

Studies on military veterans show that massage reduces anxiety, worry, depression, physical pain, irritability and tension[xxv]. Another study, conducted on nurses during work hours, shows that even simple 15-minute chair massage reduces stress-related symptoms[xxvi].

Massage can also significantly reduce chronic low-back pain, reducing the use of anti-inflammatory drugs for pain[xxvii]. Regular massage therapy is also beneficial for older adults. It produces a relaxation effect for the entire body, lowers blood pressure, decreases stress, and improves balance[xxviii]. Massage is also effective at controlling blood pressure, lowering it for up to 72 hours after massage[xxix].

Massage is one of the most effective ways to reduce your stress and improve your well-being. So why don't most people don't have it regularly?

1. Cost

Massage isn't the cheapest therapy. If you want to have a massage once or twice a month, the costs add up quickly.

There are a couple of solutions to this problem. The first, most obvious one, is decrease your spending in other areas. Give up an unhealthy habit (skip some fast food meals) and spend this money on a massage. Long-term effects of massage will be much more beneficial than short-term pleasure of engaging in a vice. Moreover, consider the future savings by preventing stress-related conditions and physical injuries.

Another solution is for both you and your partner to learn how to give each other massages. Not only will you both be able to get massages whenever you want, it will improve intimacy you share with your partner. Obviously this kind of massage won't be as beneficial as massage performed by an experienced massage therapist, but it will still lower stress and decrease pain.

There are affordable massage classes in most cities. If you don't want to spend money on taking a course, you can learn massage from online videos.

Another option is to learn how to massage yourself without the help of others. You can perform the most basic massage techniques with no equipment and little knowledge. Neck, shoulders, abdomen, arms, hands, legs, feet – you can massage all of these body parts on your own.

Massaging your back is more tricky and can't be performed properly without some equipment. You can take a ball of any size (from a tennis ball to a basketball), put it against a wall and move your body against it, relieving the tension from your lower to upper back.

Self-massage is definitely not as relaxing as a proper massage, but it's still effective for pain and stress relief.

My preferred choice for self-massage is using a foam roller. A foam roller is a dense foam cylinder, usually at least 6 inches (15 cm) in diameter and 12–36 inches (30–90 cm) in length. Rolling the foam roller under each muscle group until you find a tender, tense area and maintaining pressure on it for 30 to 60 seconds is extremely effective at relaxing the muscle.

Foam rolling is effective at reducing pain and preventing injuries, but it's not particularly relaxing. If you have tight muscles, foam rolling will be extremely painful at first. It's a normal reaction that will gradually decrease in intensity with each session. I suggest watching several instructional videos on foam rolling online to learn the proper technique.

For your feet and other smaller muscles, use a tennis or lacrosse ball.

2. Shame

For many people, massage has a sexual connotation. And even if it doesn't have an outright implication, being touched in a sensitive way by a stranger is awkward.

The first session can be a strange experience, indeed. However, a professional massage therapist will make you feel less self-conscious and help you relax. It's worth testing your assumptions – perhaps it won't feel as awkward as you believe. If it is, you can always learn massage with your partner.

3. Lack of time

This is the most common reply of busy people. If it's you, ask yourself a simple question – is decreased stress and pain and improved well-being worth investing one to two hours a month? How much more time would you lose if you had to go on medical leave due to stress or physical injuries?

Regular massage therapy is one of the keys to maintain your body and mind in a healthy state. Find a way to benefit from it regularly.

LET YOUR BODY RECHARGE: A QUICK RECAP

1. If you don't get enough sleep, you behave like a drunk person. Get more sleep – either by making the time to sleep longer during the night or taking a nap during the day.

2. The most time-efficient way to get more sleep and recharge yourself is to take a 15 to 20 minute power nap. If you have the time, take a 90-minute nap – it's the most powerful way to re-energize yourself during the day.

3. There are seven main factors influencing your sleep quality. To improve it, maintain a consistent sleep schedule, make your bedroom relatively cool, and make your sleep area as dark and quiet as possible. Get a new mattress if you've been sleeping on the same mattress for more than 10 years. Avoid blue light before sleep. If you can't stop your racing mind, get out of bed and write down all your thoughts. Avoid caffeine 7 to 8 hours before going to sleep. Don't eat heavy meals two to three hours before going to sleep.

4. Fasting rebuilds dysfunctional components of your body. It has a positive effect on your cardiovascular health and your brain. It can help lose weight, decrease bad cholesterol levels and triglyceride levels.

5. Three most common approaches to fasting are: fasting for 16 to 20 hours every day and eating in a shorter window, abstaining from food for 24 hours once or twice a week, and having a 36-hour fast by skipping an entire day of eating.

6. Massage therapy is one of the most effective ways to battle stress and recharge your body. Consider having a massage at least once a month to decrease your stress, alleviate pain and prevent stress-related disorders.

7. Self-massage is a viable alternative if you can't afford a professional massage. Foam rolling is the cheapest and most effective option.

Chapter 3: Get Away from It All to Regain Energy

Noise has become an everyday companion in our lives. If you live in a major city, it's even worse. Add to that crowds of people, cars and other highly-stimulating elements of the environment.

There's no wonder that living in a city roughly doubles the risk of schizophrenia, increases the risk of anxiety disorders by 21%, and the risk of mood disorders by 39%[xxx]. Despite the crowds all around us, we feel completely alone.

Am I suggesting moving to the country? Not necessarily. Though research shows it can improve your well-being, there are strategies you can use to reduce your stress without losing the benefits of urban living.

How to Reduce Your Stress by Reducing Noise Pollution

Noise pollution is one of the most impactful sources of stress. Research by insulation firm

Rockwool found that 38% of people living in Great Britain – population of 17.5 million – have been disturbed by noisy neighbors in the past two years[xxxi].

Loud music, TVs, singing, slammed doors, barking dogs, crying children, musical instruments, do-it-yourself jobs – all of these things contribute to increased noise that leads to stress. For 6% of people included in the research, the problem is so bad they feel like prisoners in their own homes.

Increased noise also leads to sleep disturbance, which in turn leads to decreased sleep quality and health dangers associated with sleep deprivation.

Reducing the noise level of your surroundings – especially in your own home – can help you decrease your stress levels and recharge your batteries after work.

Many factors for noise – the sound of the traffic, commercial and industrial noise nearby, the sounds coming from the building in which you live – are outside your control unless you decide to move out. However, there are still several techniques you can use to control noise.

One of the simplest ways to soundproof your home is to invest in a high-quality thick carpet. Hardwood floors send sound reverberating through a house while carpets muffle it. Bare walls produce similar effects to hardwood floors. Consider investing in blinds, curtains, wall hangings, or canvas paintings and putting bookshelves and upholstered furniture against the walls.

Old appliances are another culprit of noise. Refrigerators, dishwashers, laundromats, and dryers can produce so much noise that they disturb your sleep. Insulating the walls of rooms with these appliances helps reduce noise. Investing in new, more energy-efficient, and quieter appliances will produce noticeable effects.

If your house is particularly noisy, consider a consultation with an insulation specialist. Proper insulation will both reduce your energy bills as well as noise levels. Solid doors, double-paned windows, caulking existing windows, placing shutters inside the windows, insulating plastic pipes, sealing all cracks or openings in walls and doors – all of these home improvement ideas can tremendously reduce noise pollution.

If you live in a single-family house with a backyard, consider planting trees and hedges. Thick conifers and broadleaved evergreens are most effective at blocking noise all year round. They will also provide privacy, turning your immediate surroundings into a more peaceful oasis.

Keep in mind a solid wooden, concrete or vinyl fence is always a better noise-blocking solution than a hedge, though a hedge will provide a psychological relief (noise isn't as annoying if you can't see the source of it).

Wearing noise-canceling headphones while working can help you block the external noise. You can also wear ear plugs if you prefer silence. Sound machines generating white noise or the sound of ocean can be a good option to replace the annoying sound of traffic with something more calming.

Your habits also influence the level of noise around you. Consider not turning on music, the radio, or a TV at least once a week. Sit in silence and enjoy your meal or read a book without distracting yourself with noise.

Escape to Nature to Recover

In addition to soundproofing your house, consider making it a regular habit to escape to quiet, tranquil places, ideally away from the civilization.

Studies show that living in proximity to green space is associated with higher well-being[xxxii]. If you don't live near green spaces, it's even more important to visit them at least once a week. Studies also show that being in nature is rehabilitative for people experiencing high levels of stress[xxxiii]. Social interactions in nature were also found to be effective at stress reduction. Contact with nature also enhances health and prevents illnesses[xxxiv].

In Japan, a visit to a forest has its own name – *Shinrin-yoku*, a forest bath. Studies on forest bathing show that forest environments reduce cortisol (the stress hormone), lower pulse rate, and lower blood pressure[xxxv].

There are many more studies proving how beneficial spending time in nature is to human health.

Science shows that being in nature regularly is without a doubt one of the best ways to prevent stress and reduce current levels of it.

Although even a walk in the park can provide you with some relief from the hustle and bustle, escaping to a forest or any other kind of wilderness is a better choice. Wild places are quieter and more remote than urban green spaces, meaning they're more restorative.

It goes without saying you shouldn't use electronic devices when you're recharging your batteries away from the world – maybe except for using an e-reader to read a book in silence.

It's worth noting that the best way to benefit from being in nature is to combine it with physical exercise.

Studies show that outdoor activity is more effective at improving mood than indoor activity. As the researchers note, benefits include "greater feelings of revitalization and positive engagement, decreases in tension, confusion, anger, and depression, and increased energy ... Participants reported greater enjoyment and satisfaction with outdoor activity and declared a greater intent to repeat the activity at a later date[xxxvi]".

Spending time outdoors in the sunlight begins a process of vitamin D production. A deficiency of this vitamin has been associated with depression[xxxvii]. Getting a lot of natural light will also help regulate circadian rhythm and help improve sleep quality.

There are many ways to spend more time in nature if you're willing to make some changes to your daily or weekly schedule. Here are some ideas to get you going:

1. Take a hike in the woods. Take a blanket, lie beside a tree, and look at the sky.

2. Go for a boat ride or have a kayaking trip on a nearby lake or river.

3. Spend more time in your backyard. Plant flowers or vegetables, lie on your recliner, or take a nap in a hammock.

4. Jog at the beach, ideally away from public beaches where you can get away from the noise and human activity.

5. Go camping. Spend a night in the wilderness or in your own backyard.

6. Go on a bike ride. A bike will get your blood pumping and let you explore places you can't reach in your car.

7. Take up a sport or a hobby that requires you to spend time in nature. Surfing, rock climbing, scuba diving, horseback riding, skiing, snowboarding, mountain biking, rafting, birdwatching, and snorkeling are just some of the ideas you can consider.

Play

Nature has a way of reducing tension and bringing out our inner child. Don't feel stupid chasing after a Frisbee like a 12-year old or lying in the grass and looking at the sky. It's the act of letting go and reminding yourself of the kid inside you that helps reduce tension and look at your problems from distance.

Charlie Hoehn, bestselling author of *Play It Away: A Workaholic's Cure for Anxiety*[xxxviii] claims that acting like a child and allowing ourselves guilt-free play is the most effective way to reduce anxiety.

As he notes in his blog post on the blog of Tim Ferriss, guilt-free play with friends was one of the most effective techniques that have helped him go back to his normal, relaxed self in less than a month[xxxix].

When was the last time you took a genuine break and played with your friends? I'm not talking about drinking coffee together. I'm talking about the fun stuff – things like playing with an Aerobie, improv comedy, rock climbing, shooting range, billiards, going on a road trip, jumping on a trampoline, and so on.

Schedule at least a few sessions of guilt-free play a week to reduce your tension and enjoy time with friends.

GET AWAY FROM IT ALL TO REGAIN ENERGY: QUICK RECAP

1. Noise pollution leads to increased stress. If you live in a city, it's even more important to soundproof your home as much as possible.

2. Some of the most effective ways to reduce the noise in your house include: investing in thick carpets, covering walls with canvas paintings or hangings, and using blinds and curtains. Old appliances can also generate a lot of noise. You can either insulate the rooms in which these appliances operate or buy new, quieter, and more energy-efficient appliances.

A consultation with an insulation specialist can help you find other sources of noise in your house. Proper insulation will reduce the noise levels and your energy bills.

3. If you live in a single-family house, consider installing a fence, and planting trees and hedges to block the noise and increase your privacy.

4. Wearing noise-canceling headphones, ear plugs, or using sound machines are also effective at

battling noise pollution. Sound machines are particularly useful for houses in which you can't block the external noise any further. It's better to listen to the sound of the ocean or white noise than the sounds of traffic.

5. Being in nature is immensely beneficial for your mental health, especially if you suffer from high levels of stress. Escaping noise and the highly-stimulating urban surroundings can help you decrease your stress and prevent future stress-related disorders.

6. Physical activity and social interactions in natural settings are two ways to increase the healthy effect of nature on your well-being.

7. Most of us suffer from a deficit of guilt-free play. Grab your friends and do something fun you haven't done for a long time (or ever). It's one of the most effective ways to reduce anxiety.

Chapter 4: Let It Go

Often, the biggest stressors in our lives are in our heads instead of coming from our immediate surroundings.

A boss who yelled at you for making a mistake often doesn't even remember it the next day, while you replay it in your head for the next two weeks.

A nasty remark from a colleague who wanted to poke fun at you feels like a joke for her, while you can think about it for months and become self-conscious of whatever she pointed out.

Your mother telling you you're not perfect or you're not worthy can echo in your mind for decades, causing you unnecessary pain and stress.

Such mental stressors are much more difficult to deal with than external ones. You can block stressful noise with ear plugs and get rid of the problem right away, but you can't just stop having these negative, stressful thoughts. Or can you?

How to Stop Torturing Yourself

The stressful thoughts in your mind have power over you only if you brood over them. Engaging in this destructive behavior is a sure-fire way to increase stress and never get them out of your mind.

One of the most effective ways to handle this problem is to reduce the intensity of the situation nagging at your mind[xl]. If you're constantly thinking about a past situation, chances are you're intensifying it in your mind. You make the mental picture sharper, brighter, louder, more emotionally charged than it really was. How do you expect to deal with this thought if you're making it so big and bothersome?

Neuro-linguistic programming (NLP), pseudoscience or not[xli], has one thing right: our perceptions indeed affect our thinking. The more intensive the picture is in your head (and the more often you visualize it), the more stressful it is to think about it. Consequently, the first step to get rid of nagging thoughts is to reduce their intensity in your head and change the emotional association.

Let's say that every single day a picture of your boss yelling at you gets you frustrated and stressed out. You picture the veins on his neck. You hear his raised voice cutting the air around you like a knife. Your hands shake from stress. You worry that you'll be fired.

Each time you see your boss, this image is back in your head – along with all the negative emotions. You don't even have to see him – the thought constantly pops in your head, even when you're trying to recharge at home. All the stress is back, and there goes your positive mood.

To stop this thought from ruining your day, you need to break the pattern – automated behavior associated with picturing this image in your head. One of the most effective ways to break the pattern of negative thoughts is to turn them in your head into bad, ridiculous, cheap movies. Sounds strange? Perhaps, but it works.

Bring back the image of the boss yelling at you. Now give him funny-looking pink glasses. Put a fake mustache on his face. Let him wear yellow kitchen gloves and yell at you in a funny, high-pitched voice. Add funny music in the background.

Now change the perspective of this thought in your mind by looking at the scene as a spectator instead of in first person. How ridiculous does this image look? Does it break the stress in your head and make you feel more like laughing than despairing? It should. If not, add more details that will make you laugh and disassociate the negative feelings conjuring up this image brings.

Each time you feel like worrying over the image of your boss yelling at you, replace it with a new, ridiculous thought. Sooner or later, the old image will lose its power and you'll no longer get so stressed out by merely looking at your boss.

It's never the image in your head that makes you stressed out – it's your perception of it. If you change the feelings associated with a stressful situation, you can finally get it out of your head as nothing more than a bad joke.

The goal is to make an automatic association. Each time you see the image of your boss yelling at you, you have to replace it with the ridiculous image until you can't think about your angry boss without seeing him in idiotic pink glasses.

Wouldn't it make the scene less stressful and help you avoid torturing yourself by replaying this unpleasant scene?

Note that you can also use this technique while experiencing a negative situation. If you increase the intensity of the situation happening right in front of you, it will bother you later on. If you reduce it the moment it's happening, chances are you'll either not think about it at all or experience much weaker and much less frequent nagging (and you now know how to deal with that).

Get Rid of Negativity in Your Head

Nagging thoughts are caused by your default negative responses. Instead of thinking how to deal with the problem, you torture yourself by repeating it over and over in your head. Reducing the intensity of the thought can help you deal with it, but wouldn't it be better to prevent these thoughts from entering your mind?

Here's where a 7-day "Change Your Thoughts" challenge comes in (I totally made that name up). My idea is inspired by international bestselling author Will Bowen's *Complaint Free challenge*[xlii]. Bowen's challenge is about going 21 days without making a single complaint.

I suggest making the challenge a bit harder – blocking any negative thoughts entering your mind. Obviously, you can't just get rid of negative thoughts right away. Hence, the objective of my challenge is to go 7 days without letting yourself brood over negativity.

If you start worrying and don't stop, despite being aware of it, go back to day zero. If you start complaining and don't stop yourself from voicing more complaints, start again. If you start thinking about a past negative situation and make yourself feel bad instead of reducing its intensity, back to square one it is. Self-awareness is your main job during the next 7 days.

This simple challenge will help you become more aware of your negative patterns and break them before they make you feel stressed out. To make the challenge a bit easier, consider:

1. Not watching or reading any media. Media is designed to make us feel threatened. That's what sells because humans have a negativity bias[xliii], a tendency to pay more attention to negative information than positive news. Surrounding yourself with negative news will put you into a more negative state, thus making the challenge more difficult. I haven't watched news for many years, and I don't miss anything. 99% (if not more, but that's just my opinion, and not scientific evidence) of reported news have no impact whatsoever on your life. You'll learn about the remaining 1% from your friends and family.

2. Avoiding negative people. Most of us have some people in our lives who don't contribute positively to our well-being. They complain, they nag, they make you feel angry or abused. For the next seven days, try to cut these people from your life entirely.

3. Putting much more focus on gratitude. We've already discussed how powerful it is. Gratefulness has

a way of making us feel happier and looking with more optimism to the future. You can change your default response to bad things happening in your life by finding what's good about them (there's always something good) and expressing gratitude for that.

After completing this challenge, you should notice how much stress negativity brings into your life and why it's worth learning to filter your thoughts and replace bad ones with positive ones. It's not hokey self-help. It's science, backed by numerous studies[xliv].

LET IT GO: QUICK RECAP

1. Negative thoughts, such as replaying in your head how your boss yelled at you a week ago, can instantly make you feel stressed out – even when you're supposed to be relaxing. Unless you learn how to deal with these thoughts, you'll never fully recharge your batteries.

2. One of the most effective ways to stop letting negative thoughts affect your state of mind is to reduce their intensity. By turning the negative image into a ridiculous, absurd situation, you'll change your emotional association with the situation. When you break your behavioral pattern this way, you won't reinforce the thought in your head, thus making it easier to throw it away.

3. Use the same technique during a stressful situation. It will reduce its intensity and help you remain in a resourceful, positive state instead of stressing out (and replaying the situation in your head many times later on).

4. Prevent future negative thoughts by taking a 7-day "Change Your Thoughts" challenge. Become

more aware of your negative thoughts and deal with them instead of brooding over them. It will help you change your default responses and go from a person who stresses out over a past situation to a person who forgets about it seconds after it happened.

Chapter 5: Seven Habits to Reduce Stress

Throughout the previous chapters, we covered numerous habits and actions that can help you step away and recharge your batteries.

In the last chapter of this part, I'd like to share with you seven less obvious ideas to reduce stress we haven't discussed yet. These habits aren't so complicated that they need a separate chapter, but implementing them in your life can still provide you with many benefits.

Manage Your Stressors

Weekly or monthly assessments of your personal life can help you pinpoint potential ways to improve your life. First, find what stresses you the most on a regular basis.

Set your timer for five minutes and write down as many stressors in your life as possible – no matter how small or big they are. Write down both your pet peeves and challenges that have been stressing you out lately.

Now that you have your list, identify which are most stressful. The 80/20 rule says that 80% of the outputs come from 20% of the inputs. When applied to stressors, 20% of the stressors bring 80% of the stress. Reorder your list to start with the most powerful stressors. Then come up with ideas to reduce or eliminate the first five problems.

If it's a person and his or her behavior, communicate how it makes you feel and what you can both do about it to help each other.

If it's a specific part of your environment (noisy neighbors), either find a way to put an end to it (ask them to be more considerate of their neighbors), or, if you can't change it and it's a powerful stressor, move out (obviously it's not an easy decision, but worth considering if stress poisons your life).

If it's a certain errand (like waiting in a line when shopping), consider delegating it to someone else. Nobody said you have to do everything.

If you aren't sure which stressors are the most powerful, ask yourself which stressor you'd like to eliminate from your life if you had a magic wand. Reorder your list one by one, asking yourself the same question after eliminating each stressor.

You can also give yourself a score from 0 to 10, 0 meaning extremely stressed out and 10 meaning perfect calmness and ask yourself what needs to change to improve your score. Sometimes one simple change can take you from 4 to 7.

Making such a list will help you prepare an actionable plan to reduce stress in your life.

Do It Now

Procrastination is not only bad for your productivity, but also for your mental health. Studies show that it's associated with lower self-compassion and higher stress[xlv].

Putting things off is like preferring to avoid short-term pain now in exchange for even bigger pain later. You prefer not to get your teeth checked today in exchange for excruciating tooth pain several months from now. When put this way, it's irrational to engage in this behavior, yet it's still a huge struggle for many people to stop putting things off.

There are several ways to get rid of this habit and create a habit of doing everything now.

1. Ask yourself if the tasks you're postponing are essential at all. It's likely you have a tendency to put off tasks that are irrelevant and nothing bad would happen if you didn't do them. The problem doesn't necessarily have to lie in postponing – it's just a case of trying to do too much.

2. Break down your tasks into smaller parts. If it takes you two or more hours to perform a specific task, break it down into four or more smaller tasks. It will sound less overwhelming, so you should feel less resistance.

A variation of this approach is to ask yourself if you can do something just for the next minute or two. Once the time is up, ask yourself if you can do it for another minute or two. Soon, you'll get engaged in your task and keep going.

I'm a huge fan of the Pomodoro technique[xlvi], a time management method that suggests breaking down work into 25-minute sessions separated by short 5-minute breaks. If I have a job to do, I use pomodoros to make the task much less overwhelming. It also helps deal with distractions, because each 25 minutes you're allowed to indulge for 5 minutes. Short sprints work much better than long marathons.

3. Change your feelings about procrastination by making it much more painful to put things off.

As painful as putting things off can be, it's not painful enough if you're still doing it. What if you punished yourself each time you didn't complete a certain task on time? Wouldn't it put enough pressure on you to start now rather than postpone it for later?

I used this technique when I made a goal to start waking up at 6 AM. I told myself I would have to pay 100 bucks for each morning I didn't wake up at 6 AM. After 30 or so days, I didn't need this motivation longer – the change was permanent. I highly doubt I would achieve it without setting stakes. $100 fees for oversleeping weren't worth it.

Show Up Early

Being late, especially for an important meeting, is one of the most stressful events that can happen on a regular basis in your life. Things happen, and it's not always your fault you're late. However, it doesn't mean there's nothing you can do about it.

What if every single time you mentally switched the time of the meeting to five to ten minutes earlier? Even if you were running late, five to ten minutes should be enough to cover you.

If you're afraid you'll waste your time by arriving earlier, always have some small tasks set aside for periods of waiting. Five minutes is enough to reply to a few short emails, make a list of things to do for the next day, make a quick call or do any other type of a brief activity that doesn't require more than a few minutes at most.

Single-Task and Focus

Research conducted at Stanford University shows that multi-tasking is less productive than doing things one at a time. Moreover, distracted people can't pay full attention, recall information, or choose the next task to perform[xlvii].

As one of the researchers said, "They [multi-taskers] couldn't help thinking about the task they weren't doing. The high multitaskers are always drawing from all the information in front of them. They can't keep things separate in their minds."

Guess how calm and in control you feel if you can't even keep your thoughts separate.

British psychologist Glenn Wilson conducted a survey of around 1000 HP workers on the negative effects of "infomania," misusing distracting technology[xlviii]. His findings show that technological distraction diminishes IQ by 10 points. Moreover, distraction dramatically increases stress – from self-reported 2.75 on a 0-10 scale to 5.5 for males and 4.75 to 6.75 for females.

Learn to take tasks one by one and avoid distractions. Silence your phone, log off social media sites and focus on the task at hand. You'll gain more clarity, perform the tasks more quickly and with less stress.

If productivity and a clearer mind still don't persuade you to start single-tasking, think about your friends and family. If you multi-task around them, you never give them your full attention. How would you feel if you always had only half of someone's attention?

Have an Open Schedule

"I'm so busy," "Let me see if I can fit you in my calendar," "Call me later and I'll see if I can make it" are all common responses when trying to hang out with someone spontaneously. What happened to unplanned meetings? Where's "Sure, when?" Why is it so hard to get people to commit to a meeting?

Have you ever felt like a prisoner of your schedule? If so, it's high time to regain control over this aspect of your life and open up your schedule. Go back to the times when you didn't have such a restrictive schedule. Weren't you more relaxed? Didn't you enjoy the time spent with friends more?

You'll say, "Yes, but it was different then. I'm an adult now, I have too many obligations." I say, it all depends on you. It's not like there's someone who controls your schedule and tells you to book your entire day.

Why not schedule (what an irony) at least one or two hours each day for spontaneous activities? Could you loosen up your day so that you'll have more flexibility to spend time with other people?

As long as you're not a planning freak, opening up your schedule will reduce tension in your life and make you feel more in control of it.

Let Go of Control

We give ourselves a lot of unnecessary stress by being control freaks. If you constantly obsess over controlling every single aspect of your life, you take stress with you wherever you go – just like the nagging, negative thoughts.

Giving away control is a skill you can master by gradually letting go of it. Start with something simple. Let someone else clean your home for you. Stay silent and don't tell this person she's doing it the wrong way. Delegate a simple task at work to a colleague and don't comment on how she's doing it. Ideally, don't watch how this person is performing the task –

just accept the results no matter how they were achieved.

To open your mind, seek different approaches of doing things. Observe how others do things and try to learn from them. Listen instead of giving orders. Work with people instead telling them what to do.

Relinquishing control can be a great way to reduce stress, free up your schedule, and enjoy your life more – knowing that others will take care of the things just as well, if not better, than you.

De-Clutter Your Surroundings

Scientists at the Princeton University Neuroscience Institute found that clutter diminishes your ability to focus and limits your ability to process information[xlix].

Chaos in your environment contributes to stress and distraction. A simple habit of cleaning your desk and limiting it to a few key items can tremendously increase your concentration when working. It will also shift your attention from the items around you to the essence of the task at hand.

The same applies to your home environment. If you have too much stuff in every room, the chaos in your surroundings can make you frustrated and stressed.

Consider throwing away all the things you no longer need – starting with the rooms you visit most often. You'll be surprised how much peace of mind you can gain by simply restricting the amount of physical junk around you.

SEVEN HABITS TO REDUCE STRESS: QUICK RECAP

1. Manage your stressors. Identify what makes you most stressed and find a way to eliminate it from your life (or at least reduce its impact). According to the 80/20 principle, just 20% of the stressors bring 80% of the stress. Discover your top stressors and make a list of solutions to get rid of them.

2. Procrastination gets more stressful the more things you put off. If you can't motivate yourself to do something, don't do it. If you have to do it, delegate it. It's usually not procrastination you're dealing with – it's just that you're trying to do things you don't need to do in the first place.

3. Show up early. Develop a habit to always be at least five minutes early. Being in a rush is a sure-fire way to get stressed out. Don't be afraid that you'll lose five minutes by being early for each appointment. If you don't want to take a break during this time, you can always pull out your phone and reply to emails or do other small tasks.

4. Single-task. Multi-tasking doesn't work, and the more things you're trying to juggle at the same time, the lower the quality of your actions. Multi-tasking affects your productivity, causes stress, and can hurt the people closest to you when your lack of attention shows lack of care.

5. Have an open schedule. If you pile obligations on top of obligations, you'll feel like a prisoner. Unless you thrive under pressure and love having every single hour of your day planned, loosen up your calendar. Schedule at least one or two hours each day for unscheduled meetings or just for spending time in solitude.

6. Stop trying to control things over which you have little or no control. It leads to unnecessary stress, especially if you're trying to control other people. Learn how to let go of control by gradually releasing it – starting with simple tasks, and then moving on to things that would usually turn you into a certified control freak.

7. Physical junk around you can lead to increased stress. Clean your desk, get rid of clothes you no

longer use, throw away all the old stuff you thought would be useful one day. It's much less stressful and distracting to work in an organized environment than a cluttered one.

Epilogue

I created this book to help you discover some of the most effective ways to handle stress and recharge your batteries. Instead of sharing obvious advice, I strived to provide tips that you might not have thought about. To reiterate the most crucial advice, here are five key things to remember:

1. If you start your day on the right note, it will unfold in the same exact way. If you start it by rushing and stressing out, you'll be in a reactive state of mind during the entire day. Guess what your chances of feeling good and slowing down during the day are if you can't even control your first waking hour.

2. Your body needs to recharge if you want to reduce your stress and feel better. In addition to the obvious advice of eating healthy and exercising regularly, remember about:

- getting enough sleep (or improving your sleep quality if you feel tired despite getting enough sleep),

- giving your digestive system a break by fasting (not necessary, but worth experimentation),

- letting your muscles relax by massage or foam rolling.

3. Noise is a major source of stress for many people, particularly those living in large cities. If it's a factor in your daily life, come up with ways to make your surroundings quieter. Escaping to nature is one of the ways to recharge your body away from noise and other people.

4. Don't let negative thoughts harass you every single waking hour. Reduce the intensity of past stressful situations in your head and filter negativity in your life. The more positive your surroundings are, the less negative stress you'll feel on a daily basis.

5. Manage your stressors. If you aren't sure what exactly makes stresses you, what are your chances of fixing it? Assign scores to each stressor and come up with ways to reduce or eliminate each.

If my advice helps you reduce stress and inspires you to free up at least a few hours each week to spend enjoying yourself, I'll be more than happy.

Few things are worse than living an overly busy and stressful life. You owe it to yourself to slow down and recharge your batteries.

Bonus: How to Get Results without Being Busy

If you're wondering how you can still achieve a lot if you stop working so hard, this bonus chapter is for you.

Busyness and the pressure to work longer than your peers turn everything upside down. The more overtime you put in, the less effective you are (past 55 hours per week, you're just wasting time[1]).

Yet, so many people wear it as a badge of honor – "I work 60 hours per week, so I'm a very hard-working and productive man." What a shame that forty, if not more, of these hours are spent doing tasks that produce little to no results.

It all starts with…

The Time Delusion

More and more jobs in today's world are about providing results, and not just putting in hours. However, the mindset hasn't shifted yet – people are still paid for hours worked, and the more hours you work, the more productive you're considered to be.

Just try to tell others you're working four hours a day and see their reaction. It doesn't even matter if you achieve the same, or better, results, than they do – it's just maintaining the image of today's successful, hard-working person that's important. Results be damned. Quantity over quality!

It's easy to see why most people conform and focus on hours worked instead of their real effectiveness. If you stop working so hard, you'll be ostracized. If you're working for someone else, you'll get fired, or you'll just be given even more work (even if you accomplish more in four hours than your colleagues in twelve).

Since I've been an entrepreneur my entire life, I can't speak of how to deal with bosses and corporate rules – this is something you need to figure out on your own, based on your knowledge of how your company operates.

A survey of 2,000 office workers conducted by management software developer AtTask and market research firm Harris Interactive[li] shows that half of an employee's hours at the office are spent doing other things than her primary job duties.

That's at least twenty hours a week wasted at work you could have spent preparing healthy meals, enjoying time with your friends and family, or learning new skills.

Regardless if you're an employee or an employer, consider noting down what you're doing during the day to find out when you're most productive. How much time do you spend actually working? Then work on your most important tasks during the hours when you're most productive.

For maximum productivity while working minimum hours, set short deadlines. Parkinson's law says that work expands to fill the time available for its completion.

If you give yourself a week to accomplish something, it will take you a week to do it. If you give yourself three days to do it, you'll accomplish it in three days (while wasting much less time).

If you want to stop being busy, identify your magic hours and cut away the unessential tasks to achieve more in less time. One of the keys to achieve this outcome is to…

Think More, Act Less

It's not the amount of action you're taking that's important. It's the action, and its significance (or lack thereof) that's important.

I have a simple rule in my life that dramatically reduces the amount of time spent on useless tasks. I just ask myself what action I can take to render other, smaller tasks unnecessary.

For instance, would you like to become more productive? You can use all kinds of complex productivity systems you want, but you'll get the most benefit from following the same routine every single day. Why spend an hour categorizing your tasks (most of which aren't even necessary) into several different groups if you could just pick one key thing and work on it first thing in the morning every single day?

Shift your focus from action to getting results, and don't act until you have a clear idea of what action will bring the most results.

Free Yourself from Obligations

We all have to juggle several roles on a daily basis. Employee or business owner, spouse, parent, community member – these are just a few of the roles most people have to perform every single day. Add to that various errands you need to run each day, and you're so busy that you need to work overtime and steal away precious time previously reserved for recharging.

If you have a means to do it, free yourself from some of the obligations by delegating them to someone else. Services like Taskrabbit can help you find another person who can take care of minutiae for you – clean your house, buy groceries, plan an event.

If you can afford it, it's not extravagance or snobbism. By hiring other people to perform these tasks for you, you free up your time to perform more important tasks – either at work or in your personal life (spending more time with your spouse, playing with your kids, or just going for a bike ride or reading a good book). Plus, you've given them an opportunity to make money.

Make Fewer Decisions

Due to decision fatigue, the more decisions you make, the lower the quality of those decisions[lii]. Since busy people tend to make more choices, they're more prone to suffer from decision fatigue.

This phenomenon affects every aspect of your life –your productivity (whether you'll work on the most important task or dilly-dally), your health-related choices (whether you'll go with a greasy burger or a healthy salad), or your purchasing decisions (whether you resist the temptation to buy something you don't need when it's deeply discounted or save money).

Reduce the number of trivial decisions you make to improve the quality of your decisions. It will take away unnecessary stress from your life, and help you make better choices.

You can either eliminate some decisions from your life altogether (e.g., by wearing the same set of clothes prepared for every specific day of the week) or let someone else make them for you (e.g., let the waitress pick the meal for you at the restaurant).

If you need to make big decisions, make them in the morning while your decision making capabilities haven't been decreased yet[liii].

HOW TO GET RESULTS WITHOUT BEING BUSY: QUICK RECAP

1. Focus on the results, not the work in itself. People who tend to focus on the hours they work pay less attention to the results they're getting, thus working for the sake of work (and wasting a lot of time).

2. Less busyness and more accomplishment starts with self-awareness. Note down what you're doing during the day to find out when you achieve most results and when you waste time. Then focus on working on the most important tasks during your most productive hours.

3. Set short deadlines to reduce the amount of time reserved for slacking. The sooner you get it done, the less time you'll lose (and oftentimes, the better your results will be as you'll apply much more focus when working).

4. Before you take an action, ask yourself what action you can take to render other, smaller tasks unnecessary. You can stop doing a lot of time-

consuming tasks if you pick the right, key activity to perform.

5. Consider outsourcing some of the least important tasks to someone else. Activities like cleaning, shopping, or planning events take up a lot of time which you can spend pursuing other, more meaningful things.

6. Make fewer decisions in your life or let someone else make them for you. The more decisions you make, the lower their quality and the more unnecessary stress you put on yourself.

Download another Book for Free

I want to thank you for buying my book and offer you another book (just as valuable as this book), *Grit: How to Keep Going When You Want to Give Up*, completely free.

Visit the link below to receive it:

http://www.profoundselfimprovement.com/relax

In *Grit*, I'll share with you how exactly to stick to your goals according to peak performers and science.

In addition to getting *Grit*, you'll also have an opportunity to get my new books for free, enter giveaways and receive other valuable emails from me.

Again, here's the link to sign up:

http://www.profoundselfimprovement.com/relax

Could You Help?

I'd love to hear your opinion about my book. In the world of book publishing, there are few things more valuable than honest reviews from a wide variety of readers.

Your review will help other readers find out whether my book is for them. It will also help me reach more readers by increasing the visibility of my book.

About Martin Meadows

Martin Meadows is the pen name of an author who has dedicated his life to personal growth. He constantly reinvents himself by making drastic changes in his life.

Over the years, he has regularly fasted for over 40 hours, taught himself two foreign languages, lost over 30 pounds in 12 weeks, ran several businesses in various industries, took ice-cold showers and baths, lived on a small tropical island in a foreign country for several months, and wrote a 400-page long novel's worth of short stories in one month.

Yet, self-torture is not his passion. Martin likes to test his boundaries to discover how far his comfort zone goes.

His findings (based both on his personal experience and scientific studies) help him improve his life. If you're interested in pushing your limits and learning how to become the best version of yourself, you'll love Martin's works.

You can read his books here:

http://www.amazon.com/author/martinmeadows.

© Copyright 2015 by Meadows Publishing. All rights reserved.

Reproduction in whole or in part of this publication without express written consent is strictly prohibited. The author greatly appreciates you taking the time to read his work. Please consider leaving a review wherever you bought the book, or telling your friends about it, to help us spread the word. Thank you for supporting our work.

Efforts have been made to ensure that the information in this book is accurate and complete. However, the author and the publisher do not warrant the accuracy of the information, text and graphics contained within the book due to the rapidly changing nature of science, research, known and unknown facts and the Internet. The author and the publisher do not hold any responsibility for errors, omissions or contrary interpretation of the subject matter herein. This book is presented solely for motivational and informational purposes only.

---

[i] *National Vital Statistics Reports*, Volume 61, Number 4.

[ii] Goyal M., Singh S., Sibinga E. M., Gould N. F., Rowland-Seymour A., Sharma R., Berger Z., Sleicher D., Maron D. D., Shihab H. M., Ranasinghe P. D., Linn S., Saha S., Bass E. B., Haythornthwaite J. A. "Meditation programs for psychological stress and well-being: a systematic review and meta-analysis." *JAMA Internal Medicine* 2014; 174 (3): 357–68.

[iii] Emmons R. A., McCullough M. E., "Counting Blessings Versus Burdens: An Experimental Investigation of Gratitude and Subjective Well-Being in Daily Life." *Journal of Personality and Social Psychology* 2003; 84 (2): 377–389.

[iv] McCullough M. E., Emmons R. A., Tsang, J-A. "The Grateful Disposition: A Conceptual and Empirical Topography." *Journal of Personality and Social Psychology* 2002; 82 (1): 112–127.

[v] Sheldon K. M., Lyubomirsky S. "How to Increase and Sustain Positive Emotion: The Effects of Expressing Gratitude and Visualizing Best Possible Selves." *Journal of Positive Psychology* 2006; 1 (2): 73–82.

[vi] Algoe S. B. "Find, Remind, and Bind: The Functions of Gratitude in Everyday Relationships." *Social and Personality Psychology Compass* 2012; 6 (6): 455–469.

[vii] Algoe S. B., Gable S. L., Maisel, N. C. "It's the Little Things: Everyday Gratitude as a Booster Shot for Romantic Relationships." *Personal Relationships* 2010; 17: 217–233.

[viii] Gordon A. M., Impett E. A., Kogan A., Oveis C., Keltner D. "To Have and to Hold: Gratitude Promotes Relationship Maintenance in Intimate Bonds." *Journal of Personality and Social Psychology* 2012, 103 (2): 257-274.

[ix] Robbins T., *Unlimited Power: The New Science Of Personal Achievement.*

[x] http://drowsydriving.org/about/facts-and-stats/, Web. April 5th, 2015.

[xi] http://www.webmd.com/sleep-disorders/excessive-sleepiness-10/10-results-sleep-loss, Web. April 5th, 2015.

[xii] Milner C. E., Cote K. A., "Benefits of napping in healthy adults: impact of nap length, time of day, age, and experience

with napping." *Journal of Sleep Research* 2009; 18 (2): 272–281.

[xiii] https://sleep.org/articles/temperature-for-sleep/, Web. April 5th, 2015.

[xiv] http://www.health.harvard.edu/staying-healthy/blue-light-has-a-dark-side, Web. April 5th, 2015.

[xv] http://www.drugbank.ca/drugs/DB00201, Web. April 5th, 2015.

[xvi] Stunkard A. J., Berkowitz R., Wadden T., Tanrikut C., Reiss E., Young L. "Binge eating disorder and the night-eating syndrome". *International Journal of Obesity* 1996; 20: 1–6.

[xvii] Alirezaei M., Kemball C. C., Flynn C. T, Wood M. R., Whitton J. L., Kiosses W. B "Short-term fasting induces profound neuronal autophagy." *Autophagy* 2010; 6 (6): 702–710.

[xviii] Mattson M. P., Wan R. (2005). "Beneficial effects of intermittent fasting and caloric restriction on the cardiovascular and cerebrovascular systems." *The Journal of Nutritional Biochemistry* 2005; 16 (3): 129–137.

[xix] Martin B., Mattson M. P., Maudsley S. (2006). "Caloric restriction and intermittent fasting: Two potential diets for successful brain aging." *Ageing Research Reviews* 2006; 5 (3): 332–353.

[xx] Lieberman H. R., Caruso C. M., Niro P. J., Adam G. E., Kellogg M. D., Nindl B. C., Kramer F. M. (2008). "A double-blind, placebo-controlled test of 2 d of calorie deprivation: effects on cognition, activity, sleep, and interstitial glucose concentrations." *The American Journal of Clinical Nutrition* 2008; 88 (3): 667–76.

[xxi] Cameron J. D., Cyr M. J., Doucet E. (2010). "Increased meal frequency does not promote greater weight loss in subjects who were prescribed an 8-week equi-energetic energy-restricted diet." *The British Journal of Nutrition* 2010; 103 (8): 1098–1101.

[xxii] Leidy H. J., Armstrong C. L., Tang M., Mattes R. D., Campbell W. W. (2010). "The influence of higher protein intake

and greater eating frequency on appetite control in overweight and obese men." *Obesity (Silver Spring, Md.)* 2010; 18 (9): 1725–32.

[xxiii] Heilbronn L. K, Smith S. R., Martin, Corby K., Anton S. D, Ravussin E. "Alternate-day fasting in nonobese subjects: Effects on body weight, body composition, and energy metabolism." *The American Journal of Clinical Nutrition* 2005; 81 (1): 69–73.

[xxiv] Klempel M. C., Kroeger C. M., Varady K. A. "Alternate day fasting (ADF) with a high-fat diet produces similar weight loss and cardio-protection as ADF with a low-fat diet." *Metabolism* 2013; 62 (1): 137–43.

[xxv] Collinge W., Kahn J., Soltysik R. "Promoting reintegration of National Guard veterans and their partners using a self-directed program of integrative therapies: a pilot study." *Military Medicine* 2012; 177 (12): 1477–85.

[xxvi] Engen D. J., Wahner-Roedler D. L., Vincent A., Chon T. Y., Cha S. S., Luedtke C. A., Loehrer L. L., Dion L. J., Rodgers N. J., Bauer B. A. "Feasibility and effect of chair massage offered to nurses during work hours on stress-related symptoms: a pilot study." *Complementary Therapies in Clinical Practice* 2012; 18 (4): 212–215.

[xxvii] Majchrzycki M., Kocur P., Kotwicki T. "Deep tissue massage and nonsteroidal anti-inflammatory drugs for low back pain: a prospective randomized trial." *Scientific World Journal* 2014; 287597.

[xxviii] Sefton J. M., Yarar C., Berry J. W. "Six weeks of massage therapy produces changes in balance, neurological and cardiovascular measures in older persons." *International Journal of Therapeutic Massage & Bodywork* 2012; 5 (3): 28–40.

[xxix] Givi M. "Durability of Effect of Massage Therapy on Blood Pressure." *International Journal of Preventive Medicine* 2013; 4 (5): 511–516.

[xxx] Peen J., Schoevers R. A., Beekman A. T., Dekker J. "The current status of urban-rural differences in psychiatric disorders." *Acta Psychiatrica Scandinavica* 2010; 121 (2): 84–93.

[xxxi] http://www.express.co.uk/news/uk/94084/How-noisy-neighbours-millions-of-lives, Web. April 6th, 2015.

[xxxii] de Vries S., Verheij R., Groenewegen H., Spreeuwenberg P. "Natural environments—healthy environments? An exploratory analysis of the relationship between green space and health." *Environment and Planning* 2003; 35 (10): 1717–1731.

[xxxiii] Ottosson J., Grahn P. "The role of natural settings in crisis rehabilitation: How does the level of crisis influence the response to experiences of nature with regard to measures of rehabilitation?" *Landscape Research* 2008, 33 (1): 51–70.

[xxxiv] Pryor A., Townsend M., Maller C., Field K. "Health and well-being naturally: 'contact with nature' in health promotion for targeted individuals, communities and populations." *Health Promotion Journal of Australia* 2006; 17 (2): 114–123.

[xxxv] Bum J. P., Yuko T., Tamami K., Takahide K., Yoshifumi M. "The physiological effects of Shinrin-yoku (taking in the forest atmosphere or forest bathing): evidence from field experiments in 24 forests across Japan." *Environmental Health and Preventive Medicine* 2010; 15 (1): 18–26.

[xxxvi] Thompson C. J., Boddy K., Stein K., Whear R., Barton J., Depledge M.H. "Does participating in physical activity in outdoor natural environments have a greater effect on physical and mental well-being than physical activity indoors? A systematic review." *Environmental Science and Technology* 2011; 45: 1761–1772.

[xxxvii] Anglin R., Samaan Z., Walter S., McDonald S. D. "Vitamin D deficiency and depression in adults: systematic review and meta-analysis." *British Journal of Psychiatry* 2013; 202: 100–107.

[xxxviii] Hoehn C., *Play It Away: A Workaholic's Cure for Anxiety*.

[xxxix] http://fourhourworkweek.com/2014/02/19/anxiety-attacks-2/, Web. April 16th, 2015.

[xl] These techniques are explained perfectly in Tony Robbins' book *Unlimited Power*.

[xli] Witkowski T. "Thirty-Five Years of Research on Neuro-Linguistic Programming. NLP Research Data Base. State of the

Art or Pseudoscientific Decoration?". *Polish Psychological Bulletin* 2010; 41 (2).

[xlii] Bowen W., *A Complaint Free World: How to Stop Complaining and Start Enjoying the Life You Always Wanted.*

[xliii] Baumeister R. F., Finkenauer C., Vohs K. D. "Bad is stronger than good." *Review of General Psychology* 2001; 5 (4): 323–370.

[xliv] Positive psychology is the branch of psychology that researches how to increase the quality of your life. Many of the findings about happiness and stress reduction – including expressing gratitude – come from positive psychology.

[xlv] Sirois F. M. "Procrastination and Stress: Exploring the Role of Self-compassion." *Self and Identity* 2014; 13 (2): 128–145.

[xlvi] http://pomodorotechnique.com/

[xlvii] Ophira E., Nass C., Wagner A. D. "Cognitive control in media multitaskers." *Proceedings of the National Academy of Sciences* 2009; 106 (37): 15583–15587.

[xlviii] www.drglennwilson.com/Infomania_experiment_for_HP.doc, Web. April 9th, 2015.

[xlix] McMains S., Kastner S. "Interactions of top-down and bottom-up mechanisms in human visual cortex." *The Journal of Neuroscience* 2011; 31 (2): 587–597.

[l] Pencavel J. *The Productivity of Working Hours*, Discussion Paper No. 8129, April 2014.

[li] http://www.entrepreneur.com/article/240076, Web. April 4th, 2015.

[lii] Baumeister R. F (2003), "The Psychology of Irrationality," in Brocas I.; Carrillo J. D, *The Psychology of Economic Decisions: Rationality and well-being*, pp. 1–15.

[liii] Danziger S., Levav J., Avnaim-Pesso L. "Extraneous factors in judicial decisions." *Proceedings of the National Academy of Sciences of the United States of America* 2011; 108 (17): 6889–6892

Made in the USA
Columbia, SC
19 January 2019